*Lord, teach us
to pray*

Lord, teach us to pray

Michael Hollings

McCRIMMONS
Great Wakering Essex

First published in Great Britain in 1986 by
McCrimmon Publishing Co Ltd
10-12 High Street
Great Wakering Essex

© 1986 Michael Hollings

Chapters 1 to 4 were originally published
in *The Universe*.

ISBN 0 85597 388 9

Cover design by Nick Snode
Typesetting by Barry Sarling, Rayleigh
Printed by Mayhew McCrimmon Printers Ltd,
Great Wakering, Essex

Contents

Introduction	7
1. Lord, teach us to pray	9
2. Taking God seriously	15
3. The need for silence	19
4. Praying together	23
5. To the Father through the Son in the Spirit	27

Introduction

The only excuse for another little book on prayer is this. More and more people are using the words of Jesus' disciples: Teach us to pray.

Anyone who is alert to the variety of religious experience must be aware that there is growth in many different ways of prayer.

Ideally, I think we should teach prayer with individuals personally as Christ did. This teaching can come from 'professional' people like priests, religious, counsellors etc. But it is most important that anyone who practises prayer should be available to help others.

This is especially important in families, where parents have a wonderful possibility of sowing the seed in their children of speaking and listening to God in prayer.

But we cannot give what we have not got. Unless we pray, we cannot help others to pray.

I just hope that adding this little book to the pile

of other books on prayer may lead one person to pick it up, read it or receive the gift of the Spirit of Jesus saying 'Abba Father'.

> Michael Hollings

St Mary of the Angels,
London W2

St Peter & Paul 1986

1

Lord, teach us to pray

When Jesus' friends asked him to teach them to pray they were taking his close friendship as a basis for their request. They knew him; they saw him pray; they wanted to be with him in this 'thing' which seemed to mean so much to him.

According to the scriptures, Jesus replied by giving his followers a set prayer which we know as the 'Our Father', or in other traditions the 'Lord's Prayer'.

Jesus' friends learnt from him. What I am putting to you is something of the same sort. I am putting to you in these few pages some notes of my personal development in prayer. This is not an ego trip! I have nothing to be proud about, because any development has been done by God.

Most of the time, I have stood in the way and protested. Perhaps he has made a little progress in me; I don't know. I often doubt it. Never mind — read on!

Very simply, I began prayer at my mother's knee, or on her lap. She taught me about God, taught me Our Father and Hail Mary, encouraged me to pray each night before going to bed.

In the present Baptismal Rite the parents of the child are encouraged to be the first and best instructors of their children in the ways of faith.

Today this commitment is profoundly necessary. It is not popular to learn by heart. To me, in relation to prayer, it is essential.

So frequently I come across children who are coming to first confession or first communion and do not know by heart either Our Father or Hail Mary. Who is doing what? Parents and teachers — but mostly parents — are you *TEACHING* your children to pray and giving them the tools for learning... the words of Jesus to his disciples, for instance?

Sadly, it is true in my experience that these basic prayers are unknown, to say nothing of others like Hail Holy Queen, the Rosary and so on. My reason for sadness is not only in the loss of these beautiful prayers in themselves, but also that when we are in certain types of distress or depression we are almost incapable of praying. At such a stage the possession of a set of words of prayer is beautiful.

Jesus gave a way of prayer through words; he

used words till his dying breath. We would be senseless to abandon this lead he has given, but also we would be foolish to neglect the need we have to *think* about him and what he said and did.

This takes us beyond words into using our minds. I personally soon found that simply saying prayers was not enough. I began to wonder. It seemed to me that when I talked to someone it was not going to get anywhere unless I also knew them a bit more and listened to them.

I discovered deeper prayer in Palestine, walking along Jesus' ways. And I found another man had gone along that path — St Ignatius Loyola, founder of the Jesuits. Wounded, immobile and isolated, his only reading matter was the bible. He discovered Jesus there and part of the fruit of his discovery was his epoch-making Spiritual Exercises.

Ignatius taught me to take scripture seriously, to read it often and to think about it. His simple, beautiful and obvious method is to take the bible, to select a passage and then to read it and think about it. This can be very fruitful — especially so if you read, think and pray regularly.

His method is to take a small passage, read it, and then set yourself 'into' it. By that I mean, picture yourself with Christ at the particular scene — Christmas night, the agony in the garden, Calvary, the resurrection. Become a spectator, assessing everything. Then bring yourself into it... what do I find? Where does it leave me? What can I do?

In fact, we all meditate in one way or another, but great value has been found in using the Ignatian or another method to lead individuals or groups into openness to the word and love of God.

If you take seriously what I am saying, then it is up to you to practise some form of both vocal prayer and meditation. A very simple way to practice the combination of vocal prayer and meditation would be to do three specific things.

Take the first joyful mystery of the Rosary; say the Our Father, the Hail Marys and the Glory Be slowly and deeply.

The first mystery, as I am sure you remember, is the Annunciation. In this mystery, we have vocal prayer — the angel praying to Mary (indeed God praying to Mary) to be mother of the Holy One — Emmanuel, God with us. And Mary praying also in her questioning and her acceptance. For us, this is the combination of vocal prayer and meditation.

Second, reflect on what Mary's response might do to your life, if you took it on. Can you and I say 'Yes' to God as she did?

Thirdly, you might like to say and ponder upon this prayer from St Ignatius' Exercises:

Take into your hands, Lord, my entire liberty, my memory, my understanding and my will. All that I am, all that I have, you have given to me. I surrender them to you. Dispose of them according to your will. Give me only your love and your grace. With these I am rich enough and desire nothing more.

2

Taking God seriously

Prayer for me at the beginning was very much confined to prayer times! I mean that I did not find the Pauline injunction to pray at all times even remotely penetrating my life.

I was brought up to say morning and evening prayers, and to go to Mass on Sundays. There was more to it than that, because routine at boarding school included Mass each morning of the week.

Somehow the overflow from those set times of prayer to the rest of life did not really occur.

One of the ways in which I began to find the link was through getting to know the autobiography of St Thérèse of Lisieux. As she recounts even her early life, she makes it clear just how much God entered her thoughts throughout the day. She, for instance, sits quietly while her father is fishing, and meditates on God and his creation.

She and her sister enjoyed keeping a tally of sacrifices and good acts. I am not terribly keen on that kind of thing myself, but give it as an illustration of her consciousness of God and her relationship to him all the time.

And so I came to the practice of always carrying a rosary loose in my trouser pocket. This acts as a reminder and is for me a very pleasant way of fixing my butterfly mind on some kind of prayer. It is not necessary to say a decade or a rosary, or even an Our Father or Hail Mary, though I often do. The mere contact with the beads is enough.

Of course, the great advantage is that no one knows that any prayer is going on and there are all sorts of odd times for it to happen — in a bus queue, waiting for a train, walking the streets. These need not be wasted, but it does mean the forming of a habit in yourself, so that the automatic reaction is to fall into prayer in spare moments.

I find that those periods when not specifically in Church praying or in my room are good for praying for people in general and in particular.

Two other people were very practical and most helpful. Brother Lawrence in his *Practice of the Presence of God* underlines the way it is possible for anyone to come to a habit of awareness through some self-discipline.

De Caussade in *Self-Abandonment to Divine Providence* uses a different but useful phrase — the sacrament of the present moment. It is comparatively easy, and I would think the trap for each of us is to spend quite a lot of time thinking of the past or of the future. Of course, these two aspects of our lives are important, but the only reality is now. I am now alive, I am now in God's presence, this is the moment God has given me to live for him.

This moment may be extremely exciting or enjoyable — absorbing. It may be just very dull, or painful. But whatever it may be it is this time now that I worship God by being his creature, by living now.

A constructive habit which leads to the positive use of the present moment is the development of short ejaculatory prayers. These do not have to be said aloud. They do not even have to be whispered. They can simply be in the mind and heart.

If you are praying for someone, your praying may be concentrating on God and the person. But the prayer could also be for the person and simply take the form of some short phrase, well used, well liked and well remembered.

Such phrases can come from scripture, or from tradition or can be made up by yourself. I use Thomas' post-resurrection phrase a lot — my Lord and my God. I love also: Lord, I believe, help my unbelief! and at the sickness of Lazarus 'Lord, the one you love is sick.'

For many there is the well-known Jesus Prayer — Lord Jesus Christ, Son of God, have mercy on me a sinner. And this can even be shortened to the name Jesus.

So you see, there are many different ways of praying. If we are taking God and ourselves seriously we should try to develop prayer throughout the day, not confining it to one particular time.

You might, if you are not already doing something like this, try today to build a habit which will take root and grow into your whole way of living.

3

The need for silence

While vocal prayer, meditation and short ejaculatory prayers will all to some extent continue through life, there is an element which is waiting quietly to be allowed a greater share of our prayer.

This is silence.

For a long time in my own prayer life I was afraid that if I stopped *saying* a prayer or specifically thinking out a passage from the gospel, I was not really praying at all.

I believe that silence in prayer is something which makes many people nervous. We tend to say 'but what shall I do?' and the answer comes back that we should simply sit, kneel or stand open to God in his presence. This answer can be unsatisfying, even terrifying.

We fear distractions, with our minds wandering off in different directions. We fear that awful things may come up out of our subconscious. We fear falling asleep.

Any or all of these things may happen — but do not fear! Meditation does not take us far enough. Our minds cannot know God sufficiently alone.

Beyond meditation, in the way I have written of it, is the prayer of the heart — deeper, more still, silent. It is like being with some well-loved person in our own experience when words are not enough, when we need to be really close and silent — in an embrace as it were — realising God's presence and his love, and responding from the heart with love.

Do you know the story of the old man who used to sit for long periods at the back of the church apparently doing nothing? He was asked what he did there. He replied: 'I look at him and he looks at me.'

I was immensely grateful when I was told that I did not have to meditate each time I had space for prayer. I was led to the old tradition of St John Cassian, the *Cloud of Unknowing*, the *Revelations* of Julian of Norwich and other writers. These show a simpler way of prayer coming from the heart and dependent completely on God.

One of our problems is that we depend too much upon ourselves and what we are putting into prayer. One of the lessons we should learn is that God wants our openness and love, shown by our presence at prayer. But he is the one who does the work. Unless we realise that, we remain too active and prevent God's spirit from developing in his own hidden way within us.

Today, some people find themselves silent before God quite naturally. Others need ways in and aids to remaining. There are various aids or techniques which may help, though none is essential.

One way is to take a short prayer or ejaculation or scripture phrase and to repeat it slowly and regularly but with gradually widening gaps until it may not be needed at all. Another is similar, only this time the short phrase is repeated more intensively and becomes a rhythm — until, though it continues, it is forgotten and the mind and heart are freed into a silence created by the rhythm.

Some people link this rhythm to breathing — perhaps breathing in on one phrase and out on the other.

Whatever way it may come, the object is the growth of deeper silence in both mind and heart.

Desire to continue with the well known or fear of the unknown are overcome by faith and trust in the love of the Lord and his desire for us to be one with him in love.

Growth in a closer relationship with the Lord in prayer calls for the realisation of God's presence in our lives always and everywhere, sustained by prayer at odd moments throughout the day. But more than this, it calls for a pool of silence within each day when we are more particularly aware of God's presence.

This period should, where possible, be for a length of time consistent with allowing the mind and heart to quieten from the hustle and bustle of the world. It may seem impossible to achieve this, but do not be dismayed! Small beginnings are worthwhile. Leave the development in God's care.

Two final things. This growth in silence is good for everyone. It is not a specialist way. It is of great benefit to our life as a whole to be still, open and silent at some time each day, stopping for a breather while the world goes by. Enter God's stillness, silence and love.

Secondly, the books I have mentioned are not difficult and not long. *The Cloud of Unknowing* is a bestseller. If you have not read them, try to get hold of one at least. I'm sure you will find it readable and enlightening.

4

Praying together

When writing or reading about prayer, it is easy to concentrate simply on individual 'private' prayer.

I want to widen this in two ways.

Catholics until recently have not been used to praying in groups except for family rosary or in the Legion of Mary and so on. I personally used to be deeply embarrassed at having to make public prayers in a group. But I learnt group prayer through contact with the Caribbean and the growth of group prayers in this country.

I now find them very worthwhile. There is a real sharing which enriches the individual prayer life. Moreover, it is a firm reason for giving time for prayer in the week. It is an appointment with God shared by others.

The second and obvious way of prayer is the Mass or Eucharist. We might be inclined to say that this is different — this is liturgy, worship of

God. That is true, but it is very real prayer including vocal prayer, praise, listening to God's word, joining the sacrifice and having the loving intimacy of holy communion.

The Mass is an individual and a congregational experience and action. In my early days, it was much more individual than today, with more silence, both by priest and people, more mystery and less sharing in either singing or holy communion.

I entered into deeper understanding and love of this liturgy in two ways.

I consider myself very blessed to have made many visits during priestly training and afterwards to San Giovanni in Italy to be with Padre Pio. For me Padre Pio's celebration of Mass was profoundly educative and deepening. He entered the prayer and action of the Mass to a quite extraordinary degree, taking the congregation with him in silent prayer and closer communion.

Then I was ordained priest and experienced the Mass from the altar beyond the altar rails. This privilege made me realise more than ever that a daily life of personal prayer is essential.

But this very offering of Mass led me to read about and discuss liturgical development over the years, so that I became more and more convinced of the need for reform and development.

I welcomed Pope Pius XII's letter *Mediator Dei* on the liturgy in 1947, when he centred the attention of people on the Mass and suggested that saying the rosary during Mass was not ideal. In many ways, Pius XII opened the way for Vatican II.

Gradually in parish life and other forms of ministry, I felt more and more strongly that those in the pew would benefit and grow individually and as a congregation or community through greater sharing in the Mass.

In the 1970s I was in Southall, Middlesex. Here there had already been development. We were able to advance involvement beyond the ordained priesthood through the introduction of readers and special ministers of communion.

There was also much engagement of young people, parental involvement in the preparation for holy communion and confirmation and a network of house Masses in different areas of the parish.

There can be no doubt that there was a sharpening of interest, a deepening of understanding and an increase of practice in individual and group prayer. All this helped to build a varied, prayerful and compelling celebration of the eucharist.

The background of liturgy is the prayer life of the priests and people. We do not always realise the importance of our participation. The Vatican II document on the liturgy says:

'In order that the liturgy may be able to produce its full effect it is necessary that the faithful come to it with proper dispositions, that their minds be attuned to their voices, and that they cooperate with heavenly grace lest they receive it in vain...

'It is the duty of pastors to ensure that the faithful take part, fully aware of what they are doing, actively engaged in the rite and enriched by it.

'The spiritual life, however, is not limited solely to participation in the liturgy. The Christian is indeed called to pray with others, but also in secret; furthermore, according to the teaching of the Apostles, they must pray unceasingly!' (*Constitution on the Liturgy*, §§ 11-12).

In this dimension, singly and together we are to welcome Jesus, the word of God, dwelling among us. Moreover, we need his Spirit to lead us forward into all truth.

5

To the Father through the Son in the Spirit

The early Christian prayer phrase was 'To the Father through the Son in the Spirit'. This Trinitarian expression was later modified, which is a pity, because it is a remarkable summary of the prayer life of the Christian.

All our prayer to be full and whole should be trinitarian — thought of in our own explanatory though insufficient wording 'three persons in one God'.

In prayer — in our whole relationship with God — we come into relationship with mystery. Much as we would like to penetrate the veil, it is not in our human power to do so. We can prepare ourselves by prayer and fasting. We can reach out for God, search for him — but we will always be frustrated or only partially satisfied.

Our danger is that we then say 'I am no good at prayer'; or we give up; or we rationalize the frustration into a shallow formula of recited prayer which remains unsatisfactory, but which we can understand as a ritual duty.

The foundation of our Judaic/Christian faith is

that God *reveals himself* to *us* — 'No one knows the Father except the Son', and 'you can only say the Lord Jesus by the power of the Holy Spirit.' Our prayer-relationship with God is not acquired, it is *given*.

Let us then look at this phrase 'to the Father, through the Son, in the Spirit'.

Jesus told his friends 'when you pray, say Our Father...' Much of his revelation in his life and preaching and in his own prayer was directed to the Father. 'My meat is to do the will of my Father;' 'Father, not my will but yours be done.' 'I will ask the Father and he will send...'

All our prayer then is directed to the Father who is the Creator, the source of life, the ground of our being. In coming to know him we touch the edges of eternity, of power, of the essence of God, of love.

But the Father, out of his love, sent his Son. Emmanuel, God-with-us, to show us the living reality of God's closeness to this world and our human existence. Jesus Christ was human — like us in everything but sin. In getting to know Jesus through meditating on the Scriptures we can become acclimatized to the truth that he lived through the experience of manhood from the cradle to the grave. He knew what it was to grow 'in wisdom and grace before God and man'. He made human relationships; he suffered weariness, sorrow, pain, rejection, joy, and the test of darkness. His life unfolded from the family circle to independence. As God-made-man he sustained the life of a human being, all the time maintaining his relationship with his Father; thus leaving the example and the lesson that true humanity needs to be in touch with the source of being, the Father, in order to be complete.

But that was not the end of Jesus' penetration of the mystery, because he also knew himself as communicating the Spirit, who comes from God and is communicated to the world in time and eternity. After Pentecost, it is the Spirit who pervades the world, leads us into all truth and reveals to us the mysteries of the Kingdom.

When we pray we need our presence and our centring on God, but for this to be alive and fruitful we need the gift of the Spirit 'poured out into our hearts'. We pray in the Spirit and he prays with us when we do not know what to say — Abba, Father.

The mystery of the trinity is a mystery of relationship. As best we can touch it, it is the mystery of God who is perfectly one in a threefold relationship — the embrace of the Father and Son in the kiss of the Spirit. Words fail to give the true sense and depth.

Jesus knew and lived the mystery of oneness with the Father, experienced in the Spirit. For us to experience the same wholeness and completeness we must let God pervade the whole of our life. Our relationship with God is not confined to this or that isolated act — times of prayer, of worship, of work, of sacrifice, of leisure. It is to be in all, through all, turning everything to good — making our life a whole.

This is the teaching of Christ and his own example. It is the teaching of the Church, in a sense, despite many things lacking in actual practice, much disruption and attack. The middle ages attempted the right synthesis. The three worlds of physical, psychic and spiritual were integrated. The economic, social, political and cultural orders were thought of as a harmonious unity in which each person was related to nature, to one another and to the divine source of truth and justice — the eternal Law.

The foundation was the monastic life of poverty, chastity and obedience. Leaving the world they mirrored the marks of Christ's life. But he lived it in the world.

The Reformation and the Renaissance broke this synthesis, accepting the material world as an independent reality which obeys mechanical laws and exists independent of the Spirit. This disintegration is vividly evident today and is the cause of the tension, violence, mental breakdown and loss of spiritual awareness in the world. It has affected the whole range of life including medicine. It has led to the abuse of nature and the threats to the environment. It has even invaded the Church.

In teaching his followers to pray, Christ set out the trinitarian pattern which meets our human life at all points and depths in order to make each of us one whole person. We are directed to pray to the Father through the Son and in the Spirit. We are given the great commandment to love God, our self and our neighbour. Jesus is the way to the Father, the truth of human-divine being and the communicator of his life-giving Spirit.

The human being needs the spiritual dimension in order to grow into a whole person. The danger of the Church leaders emphasising too much the legal, administrative and financial side of her existence is real and it rubs off on all of us... The Kingdom of God is here and now — within us in the depth of our being, and all round us, as the Spirit pervades the world. But we can allow the Spirit to be blocked in our own lives. We can be unconsciously eroded by materialism and rationalism, pooh-poohing faith and trust and the expectancy of the apparently miraculous in our lives.

God has given to our human weakness the power to be his sons and daughters, to experience this sonship and to be taken into the realm of the Spirit. This is the power we need in a world where we are often powerless — the power of the Spirit not out of this world but in it, transforming the world and US.

> The world is charged with the grandeur of God.
>   It will flame out, like shining from shook foil;
>   It gathers to a greatness, like the ooze of oil
> Crushed. Why do men then now not reck his rod?
> Generations have trod, have trod, have trod;
>   And all is seared with trade; bleared, smeared with toil;
>   And wears man's smudge and shares man's smell: the soil
> Is bare now, nor can foot feel, being shod.
> And for all this, nature is never spent;
>   There lives the dearest freshness deep down things;
> And though the last lights off the black West went
> Oh, morning, at the brown brink eastward, springs —
> Because the Holy Ghost over the bent
>   World broods with warm breast and with ah! bright wings.
>
>   *Gerard Manley Hopkins*